THE POWER OF HOW

OF HOW

DANIEL J. MARKIN

ISBN-10: 1475209835
EAN-13: 9781475209839

Library of Congress Control Number: 2012907011
Create Space, North Charleston, SC
Dan Markin can be reached at: danmarkin@thepowerofhow.net

Foreward

I am of the strong belief that all of us want to accomplish great things throughout our lives, and to each one of us "great things" may mean something totally different. I hope the following pages provide you insight, applicable principles and a level of thought that will help you accomplish the things that you find most important to you.

I wrote this book for anyone who wants to make a positive change in their life. As I said earlier, "great things" means many different things to each of us. In the following chapters you will find stories of individuals that accomplished great feats. Some are on a worldwide stage and others are more like you and I, in that our accomplishments, for the most part, go unrecognized by others. Irrespective if you are a world leader or common person, we can all lead ourselves and others to greatness.

Often, the only thing that stands between us and our dreams is us. Sometimes it is difficult to find the confidence and fortitude to make decisions that will lead us to success. Too often, the fear of failure is greater than the excitement of success. We essentially stand in our own way because we allow ourselves to live in a world of fear, apprehensiveness and the belief that not achieving what we set out to accomplish will only leave us with incredible disappointment.

Taking control of our destiny is not always easy, but we have to be resolve to the fact that we are the ones that control where we are going and where we will end up. However, sometimes things happen to us on our journey of life that present us with unexpected circumstances and challenges. I hope this book will help you to not only cope with those situations, but also meet them with a blinding confidence to overcome and continue on to achieve greatness.

Before we can achieve greatness, we have to believe that we can do it. But – believing is not always easy. I have found if you apply the principles in this book and commit yourself to them, you will have a quantifiable level of success. Not necessarily because you will accomplish more measurable things (which I believe is an outcome of the application of the principles too) but you will begin to think of challenges and successes in different ways. There is success in every failure and there is victory in every setback. We have to learn how to appreciate these perspectives and apply them to future endeavors to accomplish our goals.

It is important to realize that it's not always *what* happens to us in life, but *how* we deal with the things that happen to us in life. Throughout this book I share a blend of leanings that I have received from others. The individuals in this book took control of events or circumstances that were affecting them negatively and then turned them into positive outcomes. I have found benefit in this thought methodology and I am confident you will experience great success if you think in the terms presented throughout this book.

This will not always be easy, as I ask you to look at situations and take a perspective that in many instances is unconventional to your normal thought process. But, if you are looking to make a positive impact in your life, which I am assuming you are by way of reading this book, you have to change. It is a simple fact; if you are doing what you are doing currently and not getting the desired outcome, you must change or course correct to achieve your goals. Doing the same thing over and over again will provide you with the same unwanted result.

One thing is true for all of us on Earth. We are born and eventually we will die. We are certain of our eventual outcome, however it's what we do between the time we enter and the time we exit that will determine our success.

Now is the time for greatness. Now is the time for success.

Table of Contents

A Chance Meeting

It was not so long ago that I had left a meeting and I had to call my boss and give him the bad news. I didn't close the deal and this potential customer was going to choose a different line of product from our competitor. My boss did not pull any punches when telling me how he felt. Nor was he shy when telling me about all of the opportunities I had professionally. It was an awful and all-too-familiar conversation. I would do something that my boss did not like and he would give me an earful about it. And it didn't stop there. My sister was upset about something I had said to her. My parents were upset about something else I had done. I was letting my friends down because I wasn't going to our reunion weekend. I felt like I was one disappointment after another. I was already agitated and frustrated with myself when I realized I was running late for my next meeting *and* my fuel light was on. Great! Now I have to stop and get gas; I am going to be even later for my meeting. I then picked up my phone to call my customer to tell him I was going to be late, and of course, no service. This day could not get any worse. Little did I know, my perspective on life was about to change forever.

Driving into the gas station, I was in a hurry and quite upset with the start of my day. I felt like the world was resting on my shoulders and I had all but dropped it. As I pulled up to the fuel pump, everything appeared like a normal service station. I got out and began putting the gas in my car. Waiting for the tank to fill, I decided to go into the gas station and get a soda. As I approached the station, I noticed a young man probably 19 or 20 years old, standing outside by the entrance. His sweat-shirt caught my eye. It was a sweatshirt with a Marine Corps symbol and the words "All give some, some give all." Judging by his short haircut and his physical ap-pearance, I figured he was a Marine.

I always make it a point when I see someone who is currently serving or who has served our Country in the Military, to stop and tell them how much I appreciate their service. I shifted my direction and started walking towards the young man. I weaved in and out of cars to get over to him. As I walked around the final car between us, I nearly lost my breath. This young man was missing his leg from just below the knee. I was so surprised; from a distance he looked like a well bodied young Marine. I was not prepared for what I saw and it really took me back. None the less, I was still going to thank him for his service and now obviously his sacrifice.

As I walked up to him, I said "Hello." He turned and looked at me with a warming smile and said, "What's going on." I started to engage him in conversation. I asked if he was a Marine. He stood up tall and put his shoulders back with a sense of pride and said, "For the rest of my life." I found that to be an intriguing response. I thought he may be alluding to his injury and the fact that it was going to be with him for the rest of his life. But from the pride he exuded, I was sure that wasn't his perspective. I then asked him if he sustained his injury in a conflict. He replied that he had lost his leg in Afghanistan. I told him I was so sorry that he had to pay such a grave sacrifice. He looked up at me with a huge smile and shrugged his shoulders and said, "It's just a leg. I have another one."

I almost fell over. Not only were the words that came out of his mouth impressive enough, but his body language was as if he had lost a friendly two-dollar wager with a friend. I was in awe of this young man. Here I was feeling sorry for myself because I had just lost a sale, everybody was mad at me and I had nothing to be happy about in my life. This young guy had a disability that was going to affect him for the rest of his life and he could not have been a warmer, happier person. I asked him how he kept such a positive mental perspective. He made a great point; he told me that "Bad is only bad when you compare it to something better. Bad is better when you compare it to something worse." What a profound thought from someone I felt had experienced a terrible set of circumstances. I then told the young man how much I appreciated his optimism. By this point in time, I was already late for my meeting, but I was so entrenched in our conversation, I decided to continue talking with him.

I asked what his name was. He told me his name was Marvin. I asked if he had always been such an optimistic person. He replied that he never really considered himself to be optimistic; he considered himself to be someone with a normal disposition. I asked Marvin how he found the courage and strength to have such a great outlook, when other people would have just completely given up.

He told me he wasn't always like this. In the beginning, shortly after his injury, he was very upset and mad at the world. The only thing that exuded from him was anger. Marvin said he obsessively thought about all of the things that he would never be able to do again, like running, riding a bike, and the biggest disappointment was knowing he would not be able to serve his country as a Marine anymore. He hated everybody. He said, "I was mad at everyone because they had their legs and could do all of the things that I would never be able to do again. I was pushing everybody away."

Just at that minute, an attractive effervescent young woman approached with a little girl holding her hand out. Marvin's wonderful smile started to glow once again as the little girl looked up at him and said, "Daddy, can I have this?" As she held out a handful of candy, he replied, "Sure sweetheart!" He handed the woman (whom I figured for his wife) a couple of dollars and she returned with a kiss on the cheek. He kept his eyes on them as they returned to the store.

"I was mad at her too," Marvin said. I inquired why he was angry with his wife. "I was mad because she would not leave me alone. I was so miserable that I didn't want to see her; I didn't want to see anybody. Our marriage was falling apart because of my anger and resentment. My life was out of control and all I could be was mad."

Marvin continued, "It was about four months later when my unit returned from overseas. I went to the homecoming, hoping that seeing some of my old buddies would make me feel better. When I got there, it was awful. I was upset because here came my friends walking and hugging their loved ones, while I sat in a wheelchair unable to stand, run or even walk. That was my absolute low point. Just then, I turned my head to the right to see a huge African American man in a perfectly pressed Marine dress uniform. He stared right at me from beneath the rim of his black visor. He was in phenomenal shape and was wearing the rank of Lieutenant. He looked at me for what seemed to be an eternity. He then asked me if I sustained my injury in Battle. I replied that I did. The Lieutenant asked me how long ago, and I said about four months. He then asked me how long I was going to sit there. I said excuse me? He said, *You heard me correctly! How long are you going to sit there?* I was floored; this was the first time in several months that someone was not overly compassionate and almost awkward around me."

"I sat there in shock," Marvin exclaimed. The Lieutenant's second question was, *When did you stop being a Marine?* "I did not know how to answer that question. I didn't consider myself a Marine anymore. I replied to the Lieutenant, 'I don't know'." His response was, *What? Because you lost your leg, you're just going to sit there and sulk and be mad at everyone and everything? Is that what the Corps taught you? To give up? Throw in the towel when things got a little rough?* I {Marvin} said, "No" with hesitation. *No What!* "I replied with a burst of anger 'NO SIR!'." *Good* he said; *I was beginning to think you were dead.* "It felt great; he elicited an escape for my anger that I was feeling and that I had not been able to get out for months. The Lieutenant looked at me and said, *Your life is not over, you just got dealt a bad hand, and in life you don't get the option to fold!* He then continued to stare directly into my eyes; he stepped back and pulled up the pant leg of his uniform about two inches, and I saw the bottom of a prosthetic limb." *I lost my leg fifteen years ago to an infection while I was in the Corps.* "I asked him how he was still able to serve. He replied he had not served formally since the day he lost his leg." "He then said, *I did not lose my virtues the Corps taught me when I lost my leg. I am still a Marine, and I will be for the rest of my life! If you want to find a way around this, you will; if you don't, you won't* he said in a calming voice. I was astounded. I sat up straight in my wheelchair tucked in my chin, and hailed him a brisk salute. He looked at me and returned the salute."

"From that day forward, I decided I was going to get past this." Marvin said he realized the very things he was hoping to come home to, he was pushing away. His wife, his daughter, his friends, everybody. He had hoped many a night that he would get the chance to see his wife again. He was given that opportunity and he was wasting it away.

Marvin told me he was so concerned about being angry that he couldn't see all of the wonderful things that he had in his life. His anger was obscuring his vision. All he could see was the negative because that's all he wanted to see. He was beginning to open his eyes.

"I then decided I was going to do everything that I wanted to do," Marvin said. "I just had to figure out how to do it. I was not going to be able to run with my own legs, but that didn't mean I wouldn't be able to run. My brief meeting with that Lieutenant that day in the hanger saved my life."

"I am still learning; it's not like everyday I am in the best frame of mind. I just try to be a little bit better today than I was yesterday. I look for constant improvement in myself. The improvement has to come mentally, before any kind of physical results can be expected. I am doing them hand in hand, but I can't do anything until I am committed to it upstairs first."

Needless to say, I was elated that I had the opportunity of meeting Marvin. In fifteen minutes, my perspective changed. I met someone that had it far worse than me, but had a much better outlook on life than I did. I wanted to share that outlook, but I was not sure how. After all, I was not a Marine; I was just a normal person living the day-to-day challenges of life. I was upset because nobody seemed to understand my problems and the things that were causing me trouble in my life.

Deciding to Go

S o when I returned home that night I was still very inspired about the encounter I had with Marvin. However, I wished that I too, could have that kind of optimism. My favorite hobby is aviation; it is something that I have been interested in since I was young. Needless to say, I was always reading about flight and all of the things that were associated with it. Often I read books about space travel or articles about similar topics. One day I sat down and grabbed my book about the Apollo missions and read a quote from Eldrin "Buzz" Aldren, in which he said, "The hardest part was deciding to go." He was referring to the American conquest to travel to the Moon. I stopped and started thinking about that. How did we ever get to the Moon? What an enormous feat!

A few days later I was watching television, and they were highlighting President John F. Kennedy. This program showed a clip of the President stating before the world that *by the end of this decade we will commit ourselves to sending a man to the moon and returning him safely*. I am sure that President Kennedy was not a scientist or even an engineer, and he surely did not work for NASA. How could he stand before the world and make such a huge declaration? Would this really be possible? Would we be able to get a person to the Moon and return him safely? As we all know, we did accomplish this in 1969; and as President Kennedy said, *before the end of the decade*.

An expert from President Kennedys Speech to Congress:

On May 25, 1961, President John F. Kennedy addressing a special session of Congress threw down the gauntlet. He boldly challenged the assembled lawmakers: "I believe this Nation should commit itself to achieving the goal, before this decade is out, of landing a man on the Moon and returning him safely to the Earth."

At the time of Kennedy's speech, the United States had accumulated exactly 15 minutes, 22 seconds of human spaceflight experience.

I then returned to what Buzz had said, "The hardest part was deciding to go." He was referring to deciding to go to the Moon! President Kennedy already decided that we were going to the Moon. In that instant, the bar had been set and the objective was clear. We needed as a nation to reach the Moon before the end of the decade.

It is amazing, how at that moment the mindset of our country had changed. Prior to the President's declaration, these types of statements were being made: We don't know if we will be able to invent an oxygen supply system to sustain the astronauts on their voyage to the Moon. What if we cannot design textiles that will withstand the heat from exit and reentry into the atmosphere? We are not sure if we will be able to design a communication device that will allow us to maintain contact with the astronauts.

After it was decided that we were going to embark on the voyage to the Moon, the questions started changing. They became more like this: How do we invent an appropriate oxygen system? How do we design the right textiles? How do we ensure we can communicate with the astronauts? The operative word became *how*. It was not a matter of *if*. It was "How!" It was a subtle shift in words, but a change that made all of the difference. We started to look for ways to accomplish our objective instead of timidly looking at the situation and not being sure. In short, we took control of our nation's future.

If you get nothing else out of this book, please have this take-away. Great things are accomplished by people and organizations when they think in terms of "How" instead of "If." "If" allows us an out; "How" does not.

There are two types of people in the world, the "If" people and the "How" people. The "If" people are skeptical, sarcastic, and the glass is always half empty. The "How" people are the leaders, the innovators and the glass is always half full. These are the types of people that others flock to follow. Look at some other "How" people. Dr. Martin Luther King Jr. believed that there could be equality for all Americans regardless of race. He was optimistic and clear eyed about what it was he was in search of. He truly changed the world because he decided to make a difference. He did not say I don't know *if* we will ever have equality. He figured out how to lead people to it. General Eisenhower was faced with the almost impossible task of invading Normandy, France in June of 1945. He had to determine how we would be successful. He did not have the luxury to wonder if we would prevail; he had to figure out a way to prevail.

How and if are so far apart; you are either a "How" person or an "If" person.

This made me think about my meeting a couple days earlier with Marvin. I thought back to what he was saying. I remember him saying he was upset because he didn't know if he was going to be able to run, or if he would be able to swim again. He said that his entire life changed when he quit thinking about if and started thinking about how.

For the vast majority of us, we are not faced with the enormous challenges of going to the Moon, or plagued with the sort of soul searching that Marvin had to endure. However, for most of us, the big decisions in life are things like: deciding to take a new job, possibly moving away to another part of the country or world, deciding to get married or divorced. Whatever the decision, the hardest part is making the decision, just like Buzz said about going to the Moon. Once you have decided, then you are moving forward. You will be forced to deal with the potential hurdles that you will encounter as a result of your decisions.

The hardest part is deciding, because we are fearful of making the wrong decision and fear breeds hesitation. When we are fearful, we hesitate, and when we hesitate, we don't act, and when we don't act, we stay where we are and get nowhere.

Let's go back to my earlier story of President Kennedy setting us on pace to get to the Moon. What if we would not have fulfilled our goal? What if the decade would have come and gone and we wouldn't have made it to the Moon? Would our country have fallen apart? Would we all be hanging our heads here in the 21st Century because we missed the mark forty years ago? The answer is NO! Of course not! We may have not made it to the Moon, but think about how much better off our country still would have been for making the choice to shoot for the stars. The supersonic jet engine was created in the 1960's; we had breakthroughs in all aspects of aviation and communications, all produced in our effort to race to the Moon. So even if we didn't accomplish our goal, we had huge technological breakthroughs in our effort.

Let's look at the other side; what if we would have stayed in "If" mode and never reached for more? Where would we be now? I think it is a safe assumption to figure that the USA would have made it to the Moon by now. However, we would have never realized our true potential.

The amazing thing about our goal of reaching the Moon was that we had every reason in the world to abandon that goal. Let's think about all of the setbacks we experienced during the 60's. There was the Civil Rights Movement, Cuban Missile Crisis, Bay of Pigs Invasion, and the Vietnam War, just to name a few. Through all of this strife we could have abandoned our goal to reallocate money, time and effort towards things we could have felt were more important.

We see this in business all of the time; diverting from our plan because the pieces did not fall together exactly how we envisioned. In these situations, we need to be resolve to what it is we are trying to accomplish. We need to find another way to get the same result. We need to continue to think in terms of "How," instead of abandoning our vision. True vision does not change with slight swings in sales or profitability. It doesn't change as a result of slight up-ticks or down turns in the economy.

President Kennedy said that we had nine years to put a man on the Moon. When was the last time you set a vision for yourself or an organization that was nine years into the future? How about five?

One goal that many people have on the horizon is retirement. It may vary from what age you retire, but most people are putting money away for retirement. If you have money invested in the stock market and twelve years before you want to retire it drops substantially, do you sell all of your stock and never invest there again? Probably not! You understand that it is a short-term set back; you may reallocate money in other funds to continue to reach for the goal of retirement in twelve years. You don't adjust the number of years from twelve to fifteen because you have had some misfortune. You should stay resolute to your visions and goals. Sometimes setbacks will cause us to have to make sacrifices, but it gives us and our organizations direction. As humans, we have to know what we are working for. If you don't know where you are trying to lead yourself or others, you will surely never get there.

Deciding to go affects us all in different ways. Several years ago my cousin Bryan, who is an excellent singer and songwriter, had a decision to make. His decision was whether he should stay in his small home-town in eastern Ohio, or pack up his bags and head to Nashville, Tennessee to see if he could turn his passion into his career. The difficult thing about deciding what to do was, in addition to leaving the comfort of his family and friends for the unknown, he was unsure about how good of a musician he really was. So not only did he have logistical concerns to deal with, but he also had the insecurity of not knowing if he would be good enough. Bryan thought about this for a long time; his family and friends had mixed feelings. Some thought he should shoot for the stars and others thought he should just stay put and continue to make music his hobby. Bryan often told me he almost wished that somebody would have decided for him. Unfortunately, as we all know, we are the only ones that can ultimately decide what is going to happen in our lives. Eventually, Bryan decided. Bryan decided to go!

Bryan moved to Nashville, found a minimum-wage job where he would work all day, and then would mar-ket himself to local bar and club owners and play in the evenings. This was a grueling schedule; when he was not working or sleeping, he was writing or practicing music. Bryan did this for years; and for those of us who know him, know how much he wanted this, how incredibly hard he worked and the sacrifices that he made.

After all of the hard work and several years of complete dedication to "making it big," Bryan realized this passion in life was not in the cards for him as a career. He was upset and the decision to stop pushing forward was one that he did not come to easily.

Unlike our Nation setting its sights on the Moon, and getting there, Bryan set his sights on Nashville and "making it" as a musician, but that goal was never accomplished.

It's true that Bryan did not become a household name as far as singers and songwriters go. But through his voyage and his time in Nashville, he found a job that he enjoys very much. He made many new friends, and he met the woman who would eventually become his wife. If you ask Bryan today, he will be the first to tell you that going to Nashville was the best decision he ever made. This is a powerful statement when you consider he did not accomplish what he thought he was going there to do. All of these wonderful things happened to Bryan because he decided to go. Sometimes we will not accomplish what we set out to do, but we will always be better off for "setting off" to accomplish it.

The point that I am making is that you will always be able to find a reason to not go after what you want or a reason to quit pursuing it. This is what separates the "How" people from the "If" people. It's the "How" people that will always be better off for deciding to go.

The Missing Link

So why is it that we do the things that we do? Why do we make the decisions that we make? Let's start by looking at the relationship between motivation, effort and success, and how they tie into the college experience. How is it that you can have hundreds of universities throughout the United States with thousands of students with so many different reasons for being there? The answer is quite simple, motivation. Those students are there because they are motivated to be there. The next question is, if they are all motivated to be there, then why do only about 33% of them graduate? This answer is quite simple too; they did not want to put forth the *effort* to be successful. Okay, so you may be a little confused. Conventional thinking tells us that if we are motivated, we should be successful. That is almost correct; however, it doesn't take into account the relationship between motivation, *effort* and success. Most people believe that motivation and success are proportional, and that is not exactly true.

Motivation

What is motivation? Is there such a thing as good motivation and bad motivation? We as human beings have convinced ourselves that there is such a thing as either good or bad motivation. I however, believe motivation is relative; we all have a reason to do everything that we do, but our reason for doing it is sometimes stronger than others.

I was speaking with a client some time ago and he was starting to lose weight. I asked him what he had been doing to lose the weight. He told me that he was eating better and started exercising. I asked him what motivated him to change. He said he had recently been to the doctor and learned that he had diabetes. The doctor told him he needed to lose weight or would most likely face some severe health effects. My client told me he was so scared that when he went home that night and told his wife, they threw away all of the junk food in the house and went and bought healthier food at the store.

I then met with another client a few days after that and I noticed he was losing weight as well. I asked him the same questions, I had asked my other client; wondering what his motivation was to lose weight. His answer was completely different. He was planning a vacation with his new girlfriend and he wanted to be in great shape when they got to the beach in a couple of months. Now this may seem somewhat vain; and maybe it is, maybe it isn't. But the fact of the matter was this individual was making a positive change in his life, just like my first client.

Marvin was motivated to release his anger and start putting his life back together. He realized the past years of his life were far fewer than the many more years he had ahead of him to live. He was motivated for many reasons; he had a wife and young daughter. Marvin realized that he wanted more out of his life than the anger, bitterness and resentment he was feeling towards everyone and everything. Marvin decided to change; he decided to make his life better and found the motivation that would help him accomplish his goals.

This thought of good motivation can be helpful in understanding why some people are driven to do the things they do; however, we should not characterize other people's motivation as good or bad. The reason that we do anything is motivation. If you won the lottery, would you still work? Many people may say yes, but the vast majority of people would say no! So why is work so important? Why do we get up everyday and focus so hard on doing things right? When it's a nice day outside and we would rather go to the beach, or go for a bike ride instead of work, why is it that we go?

The motivation for many of us is responsibility! We have bills to pay, or children to feed, or mortgage payments to make. That is why some of us fight the urge to stay at home when we would much rather not go to work. However, some people are not as financially obligated as others and they still go to work. Often they work because they have a competitive nature which drives them to do their very best, everyday. Either way, you are still going to work; and in most cases you're going to do your very best to keep your job. The point I am making is that we all have unique reasons for doing the things we do.

Motivation is like your fingerprint; it is unique and special to you. The interesting thing is that throughout our lives we will get to experience different kinds and levels of motivation. Along the way in life, there may be people who will criticize or judge us, even call us crazy for our reasons for doing something; and that's okay! I am sure that we have felt that about other people and some of the things that they have done.

Motivation is important. It is crucial that you understand the reasons why you are doing something. This, in most cases, will give you insight into how hard you are going to work at achieving your goal or how much you are willing to sacrifice. Nothing in life worth having can be achieved without some degree of sacrifice. This will help you figure out how much effort you are going to exert. This is the key to success. Effort is what makes people successful; motivation is the driver of effort, not success. This can be a somewhat difficult concept to understand. In my first paragraph, I talked about the fact that only 33% of college students graduate. Why do so many start and so few finish? Sometimes people think academically, it is very difficult. I tend to disagree. In my experience, college was about sacrificing the time and energy to go to class and to study. I had below-average grades in high school yet I finished college with a 3.5 GPA and two degrees because I was committed to put forward the effort to help ensure my success.

For me it was pretty simple. After high school I went to work in a factory where I assembled drinking fountains. The days were very long and sometimes we would work several weeks without a day off. However, the money was very good. This was how I helped put myself through school. I learned very quickly that I wanted to do something more with my life than continue to work in a factory. I saw very quickly that the guys with college educations were in supervisory positions and the guys that did not have the formal educations were not. I learned that the guys without the education were just as capable as the men who had degrees, but they never got the opportunity the others did simply because they did not have a college education. My second motivator was fear. I said in the last chapter, fear breeds hesitation, and that is true; but it can also breed action.

When you fear not doing the right thing or making the wrong decision, that's when you experience paralyzing hesitation. When you have fear about a place you have been or an experience you have had, it triggers the opposite response. It causes you to act. This kind of fear makes you realize, *I have been there and done that and I don't want to do it again*! Fear is a generalized word, as it should be; it can take on very different meanings and levels of concern and emotion.

I feared not having choices. I enjoyed working on the assembly line. But, what if someday I wanted to be a supervisor and I didn't have the opportunity because I didn't have a college degree? I did not want to be told that I could not do something I knew I was capable of because I did not have the piece of paper proving I graduated from college.

I believe this is the reason a lot of people go to college. It is easy for people to talk in terms of education giving you opportunity, but to see it firsthand much like I did working in the factory is entirely different.

Marvin was fearful of not living a fulfilled life because of his disability. However, he realized his life would never get any better unless he did something to change it. Motivation is a powerful thing in this sense. We forget sometimes that we control our own destinies through the decisions we make. "How" people understand at the moment we make a decision, our destiny is formed. Marvin decided his destiny was not going to be decided for him. Sure, there were some things he was going to have to work around, and it might have been a little harder for him; but none the less, he wanted a better life. He knew why he wanted it and therefore he was willing to put forth tremendous amounts of effort to achieve it.

Effort

Effort is the driver of success. This is a simple concept really—the more effort you put in to achieving an objective the more success you will experience. In other words, effort is the working part of motivation. Often, people have great motivation but they have trouble putting that motivation in to action. That action is effort. How often have you heard people say, *I really want a new job*, or *I would love to travel through Europe?* These are all statements that reveal an individual's motivation. Motivation is simply a desire to do something. Many of us express differing kinds of motivation. Motivation could also be described as a desire or an interest.

If you really want to go to Europe, you could find a way. You could get a second job or start saving more, but in many cases there are other things that you may be more motivated to do. You have to prioritize your motivation because you cannot put maximum effort into *everything* that you want or *everything* that you may be motivated to do. "How" people understand that they have to deeply examine their motivation. Why are you motivated to do something? How important is this to you? How hard are you wiling to work?

Success

As you probably have surmised by now, success is the lagging indicator of effort. The harder you work at something, the more successful you will be. Now this does not mean you will always be the best. What it does mean is you will be far better than you would have been if you weren't motivated to put in the appropriate effort.

One thing is certain; you will never reach your full potential in life with anything if you don't have a burning motivation to do it. Motivation is what fulfills us in life, doing what we love is what makes us happy; and when we are happy everything in our lives tends to be shrouded in success. The opposite is true when we are doing things that we don't like to do; many things just don't seem as good as they could be.

How many times have we seen people's lives being negatively affected by a job or their boss? When you are not eager to be in a situation, you are not going to be as committed as you should be. Commitment is effort in a different form.

When President Kennedy decided that he wanted to take this nation to the Moon, I am sure there were many reasons for his motivation. However, like we discussed earlier, the motivation to get us there was stronger than the motivation to stop the endeavor in spite of all of the turmoil our country experienced during the 1960's. I also believe when we stop or discontinue something (possibly lose interest) we lose motivation. The minute we lose motivation, we need to change course.

"How" people understand if you are not motivated to do what you are doing, you need to stop and change. Those not motivated to put in the effort to be successful will never maximize their full potential. We all know this, yet we continue to do certain things because we are comfortable. Think about that for a minute; we don't like doing something, but continue to do it because we are "comfortable." I would argue that we are not comfortable, we are just apathetic. Here is the problem with apathy. As we will discuss later, change is coming; it's constant in life. If we do not always continue to do what we are motivated to do, we will be victimized by change. If we are always doing what we are motivated to do, we will be affecting change.

"How" people understand motivation changes throughout life. We need to change with it and work hard at what we want to do and we will always be successful. When you are apathetic, you are no longer motivated. Find your motivation, like Marvin, and watch your success flourish.

Finding Good Tomatoes

Why do some people seem so accomplished and others seem like they are just kind of wandering aimlessly through the game of life? To answer this question, you first have to have a clear definition of what being accomplished is. Often we think of people that are accomplished as people who have a long list of credentials behind them, as marks of achievement.

When I think of someone that is accomplished, I think more about their perspective and how they look at the world and the many problems or opportunities in it. It is very easy to point to a problem and find all of the negative things that will come of a certain circumstance.

"How" people understand that it is quite simple to take everything at face value, to look at a situation and think, *it is what it is*, but we have to learn to see situations in an almost transparent nature. We have to be able to see through situations, especially the bad ones.

In the first chapter, Marvin talked about all of his negative thoughts and how they were his only focus for quite a while. It is normal to feel this way in life sometimes, as it can be difficult to get by many of the challenges and obstacles that are presented to us. I think it is unrealistic to believe that when we are faced with a set of unfortunate circumstances, we will completely embrace them and instantly find the positive.

I know that I would not look at losing my leg the same way Marvin did. He realized that while this was a devastating life-altering circumstance, it still provided him with an opportunity to be out of the war zone and was actually an answer to his prayers.

He wished every day that he would someday return home to his wife and daughter. He was so busy being mad; he did not even realize that his wishes were granted. He was so focused on what he did not have that he could not see the things he did. We all do this in life sometimes. We have a car, but it's not the one we want. We have a house but we want a bigger one. Whatever the case, we are constantly looking for more. We are always comparing. We have a frame of reference as to what is better or worse.

One of the most important things that Marvin said that day was "Bad is only bad when you compare it to something better." I don't know if he made that up or not, but it could not be truer. It really made me think. No matter what the circumstances, I will always have it "better" than some other person. When I first thought about this, I thought in terms of material possessions, lifestyle, etc. After I gave it more thought, I realized that it was not the "things" that would allow me to have it better than another person. It was the way and the terms in which I thought about the "things" that I had in my life. We all have plenty of "things" in our lives. Some of the things are better and some of them may be worse than other people's. The goal in finding true balance is looking through what may be pervading negatives to find underlying positives. This will not always be easy, but when you begin to do it, it will get easier everyday. Eventually there will come a day when you won't even realize you are doing it. I am asking you to alter your perspective.

Perspective

Our perspective is essentially how we view things in the world. The other day I was at the grocery store and I was watching people pick out tomatoes. Not one of them walked away with the first tomato they picked up. They continued to look through the display until they found the tomatoes they wanted. If they would have believed that the tomato they first picked up – the one that may have been soft, bruised or green, was the best one they were going to find, they would have just accepted it, put it in their cart and continued shopping. However, they did not settle; they believed that if they continued to look, they would find a better tomato. In every case they did. Now granted, some had to look much harder than others. Some people might not have as high of a standard as others, but in every case they each found something they could live with. Notice I said live with and not happy about. Sure, some of the people, maybe all of them, were thrilled about the tomatoes they found. Maybe others were not so thrilled, but I know they all walked away with something.

When bad things happen in your life, what do you walk away with? Do you just accept what you got? Would you accept the first tomato you picked up, if you didn't like the way it looked? Probably not! Why is life any different than tomatoes? If you continue to search through life's trials and tribulations, you will find reasoning and rationale you can live with. Again, not always thrilled about, but perspective that you can live with. You just have to have the resolve to find it.

It's the things that we take away from the bad situations in life that stay with us. Marvin took away anger and resentment early on; this consumed him and it negatively impacted everything he did. As awful as things may be sometimes, we choose what we are going to take out of it. Like tomatoes, we take the best of what we have and move on. We do not continue to dwell on the fact that there were no good tomatoes for months or years.

Sometimes this is very difficult. People that don't bother to look after they pick up a bad tomato will never have anything in their cart. Their carts (or lives) will be empty. Bad things are going to happen to us, our families and our organizations. You have to think of problems in the perspective of tomatoes. In a whole bunch of tomatoes, there are at least a few good ones even if they all seem bad, you just have to really search to find the good.

People that don't search for the positives or good to-matoes will forever be "If" people. As I said earlier, they are the skeptics and cynics. The alarming thing is that most people who are this way, don't see themselves like this.

Many times people wonder why they are stuck in lower-level management positions or why their careers are not advancing at the clip they desire. Often it is because they don't realize they are not looking for differing perspectives. Anyone can find the problem or downside to an idea. It's the "How" people that find paths; and when there isn't one, they forge one. A major way they do this is by looking at situations differently. This does not mean you have to "look at the bright side" per say. What I am saying is that "How" people look for differing views or abstracts to a certain situation. This is perspective. Perspective is much like wisdom. The more wisdom you have, the better decisions you make, and the more successful you will be. You gain perspective by opening yourself to differing views or theories. However, you have to be open to what you are hearing. You might not always necessarily agree, but developing a differing perspective means you will have to broaden your exposure to different views, opinions, beliefs, etc.

Marvin had to look at his situation in a different perspective. It was not easy, but before he could cope and deal with his disability, he had to look at what he did have rather than what he lacked. This is hard sometimes, because we as human beings tend to focus on our disappointments rather than our successes. Marvin said that all he wanted to do was go home and be with his wife and daughter; those were his good tomatoes. He had gotten that. Clearly it was not without tremendous sacrifice, or probably not what he envisioned, but going back to what Marvin said, "I was so focused on what I didn't have, I couldn't see all of the things that I did."

It is no wonder that people like Marvin ascend the ranks of corporate America and become the leaders in our communities. People want to be inspired. People want to have someone who will lead them through whatever difficult situation they or their organization are dealing with. Often the paths through difficult situations are hard to find. Perspective will make more readily available alternative paths for us to follow. The more we look at a situation through differing perspectives, the more we will find potential paths helping us to get around and or through the problem or task at hand. But you have to be open and you have to look. Because a path is opened through perspective, that doesn't mean you have to take it. However, I would rather see ten paths around or through a difficult situation instead of two, wouldn't you?

In order to be a "How" person you have to have a broad perspective. This is something that most of us will have to work at. It is extremely important; as it is the building block of another key component of being a "How" person.

Optimism

If we look back at some of the most recognized "How" people in history, they all have one glaring thing in common. They were eternal optimists. If we look at the Founding Fathers of our country, they wanted to create a government unlike any other in the world. They were in completely uncharted waters, with regards to separate but equal powers, a government of the people by the people, etc. They believed that our country's best days were ahead of them. This is something that many former Presidents have stated publically on several occasions. Lyndon Johnson talked of America as a great society. President Regan talked of a shining city on a hill. These were men that were faced with wars, terrorist attacks, economic uncertainty and a host of other problems. Yet, they still held to the belief that the future was going to be brighter. It is no surprise these Presidents navigated our country through some of the most trying times in our Nation's history.

Abraham Lincoln had the hardship of the South seceding from the union. More men were killed in the Civil War than all of the wars the United States participated in. It is reasonable to assume that many lives would have been saved had Lincoln accepted the South's secession. Lincoln knew that even though this was a terrible time for our Country, it would ultimately bring us closer. Did he have any way of knowing that? I am not sure, but he certainly persuaded other people to believe that. People were willing to lay down their lives for the thought of a unified country of independent states.

Perspective is the building block for optimism. Without it, you will never truly be able to lead yourself or others through difficult times. Perspective gives us focus so we can ascertain realistic optimism. "How" people believe the best days are always ahead of us.

Sometimes you will hear people talk about the "glory days." This is normal and could be useful as a "point of pride," which we will discuss in the next chapter.

However, if you are always concentrating on the great things that happened in the past, how can you focus on the great things happening now or the great things that will happen in the future?

Optimism is contagious. As I stated earlier, we all want to aspire to do better and contribute to something larger than ourselves. This could be organizational success or family success. Regardless of what it may be, it is important that we all recognize our larger aspirations. From optimism we build momentum, and from momentum we build excitement.

When President Kennedy made his statement about going to the Moon, he was optimistic about our future and our ability to get there. Once we started thinking in terms of "How," we got excited and then we started moving forward. Do you want proof that optimism is contagious? Think about this; we all know President Kennedy died suddenly in November of 1963. However, his vision and the contagious optimism that we shared as a country, allowed us to reach the Moon before the end of the decade – which was long after he passed. His optimism was fueled by perspective and the thought that our best days were still ahead of us. This helped us to accomplish our goal of putting a man on the Moon during a time of great strife and uncertainty.

It's not often that an individual's vision outlasts their term in an organization, let alone their life. How often do new organizations get new leadership and the goals and priorities of that organization change? There were presidents after Kennedy, new congressman and senators, but the goal of getting to the Moon was larger than any individual. In large part, I believe the reason this objective transcended so much time and so many people, is because we all wanted to be part of something imaginative and great.

It is impossible to be imaginative and great if we don't look for the "good tomatoes." If we are always talking about what we can't have or don't get, we will be taking time away from appreciating what we do have and what we can get.

Becoming Brave

In the last chapter we talked about how important perspective is in leading to optimism. "How" people share another revering quality – courage. This is sought by so many people; almost everyone wishes they had more of it. How many times have you thought *I wish I had the courage to do that*? Well, I have news for you. Courage is not something you are born with; it is something you have to work to have. Courage is developed. Like anything else, you will have to work towards building courage to lead yourself and others through the game of life. In this chapter, I would like to discuss how you can build your courage to unleash your "How" potential.

Passion

What is the most important thing in your life? When I say important, I mean what do you think is worth dying for? Every one of us should have something that we think is larger than ourselves. It could be a higher being; it could be our children or families. It could be our country and our freedoms. Whatever the case, there is something you feel that strongly about. We can also use the word "passion" to describe how we feel about these things. When I think of things I am passionate about, they are the things that I hold close to my heart. These are the things that develop you into the person that you are, they are the things that forge your character.

It is reasonable to think there are things you feel strongly about, but are not passionate about. It is also reasonable to think there are things you feel are important but don't feel strongly about. As you can see, most of us have a scale that at the high end is passion and at the low end is insignificance. This scale will have different factors for each of us with regard to the level of importance under each category. It is reasonable to assume the things that some people are passionate about are the very same things that other people or individuals may feel are insignificant. We see this in corporate America. The things that are absolute to the marketing person don't matter as much to the human resources professional, and vice versa. This is okay, and we will talk in a little bit about how you manage through that. For the time being let's look at our individuality.

The things that we are passionate about are the things that matter most to us. These are the things that we feel very strongly about. This is where you should look to begin the development of your courage. If we look back throughout history, those people who have demonstrated incredible courage are those who had passion for what they were working toward.

Rosa Parks refused to give up her seat in Shelby Alabama in the 1960's. She was passionate about her belief that she should be equal to everyone else. She was extremely courageous because, in her mind, her cause was absolute. I am sure you have already had instances in your life where you have stood up for somebody or something you believed in, and you felt very good about it, as you should. These are the times in our lives when we truly search our souls for what is really important to us. Some of these things we don't even think about as accomplishments, but they are the building blocks for future success.

Here is an example of one:

I had the pleasure of meeting Beth at a conference. She was telling me that she had been trying to diet for some time and could not stick with it. She said she had tried everything and was on the verge of gastric bypass surgery. Beth asked what I thought about her decision to possibly have surgery and mentioned she was looking for some objective opinions which may provide her with some new perspectives. Of course I was willing to help her.

She explained that not a day went by that she wished she was not as heavy as she was. She told me she just didn't have the resolve to lose the weight. I asked her about herself, and she began to tell me about her family. She told me about her twin daughters that were born premature and what a difficult time that was both physically and emotionally for her. She indicated that one of the little girls passed away shortly after birth. Beth stated how fortunate she was to have such a beautiful little girl, and for however brief the time was with her daughter, she had pictures of the two of them that she would cherish forever. This was a clear case of positive perspective and optimism. Even though she had been through a horrendous situation with her pregnancy and the death of a child, she still found the positive, allowing herself to be optimistic about the future.

Beth had to be courageous because she had no choice; it was hard to go to the doctor and not know what he was going to say. It was hard losing a child, and the whole ordeal was overwhelming. In this circumstance, Beth was extremely courageous for herself, her family and her daughters. This is the kind of story we hear and think, *how did that poor woman get through that?* Beth had clearly demonstrated that she had the ability to be courageous; she just needed help with transference, or as I refer to them, "Points of Pride."

Points of Pride
I asked Beth how much time she spent focusing and working on making sure her kids were as healthy as possible before they were born. She said every minute of every day. I asked her how much time she spent thinking about losing weight; she said she thought about it every day.

I then helped her see what an accomplishment her pregnancy and her children were. I told Beth, *after what you have been through, you could accomplish anything.* She didn't understand. I explained she probably felt like a victim most of the time when she was going through her ordeal. She agreed. I told her whether the ordeal was something that she willed, or was willed upon her, she had to develop courage to get through it. The characteristics were no different. She was passionate about making sure her girls had the best fighting chance possible, and she was going to do everything in her power to see that they did. She was resolve to the fact that there were going to be good days and bad days and she could not give up; she had to continue to forge ahead. She had to keep her vision in front of her (the birth of her daughters). She recalled what she was putting herself through. She was willing to literally die for her daughters.

Why was this any different than losing weight? It was clearly something she wanted, she just had not yet developed the courage to go and get it.

This happens to us all. We are truly motivated to do something, but then fear sets in, and we hesitate, and we don't move forward. Courage is not the absence of fear. There is no such thing. Anyone who tells you that they fear nothing is not telling the truth. Courage is being scared to death and doing what you have to do anyway. Every day Beth was scared about what might happen to her unborn children, but she didn't get to stop living.

Every time she had to go to the doctor she was scared of what he may say, but she went anyhow. That is true courage.

Beth now needs to take the courage she developed as a result of her daughters and apply it to her objective of losing weight.

First: She has to understand that this is going to take time; she has to keep her motivation and vision in front of her.

Second: She has to remember that there are going to be up and down days, some will be better than others. She has to focus on doing her very best, everyday.

Third: Most importantly, Beth has to remember the experience she went through with her daughters, and if she can get through that she can get through anything.

Transference is simply finding times in your life when you were courageous. It could be any situation that you are proud of. Then, you have to apply the same principle to the new objective.

Sometimes in our lives it is easy to forget these instances. Marvin had always embraced the virtues the Marine Corps instilled upon him. If it weren't for the

Lieutenant that day in the hanger, these virtues might not have returned to the forefront of his mind. This man was in a war zone. He left his family and friends, traveled to a foreign land, and was shot at. Even after all Marvin had been through, he could not find a point of pride. This made it difficult for him to find the courage to move forward and overcome his disability.

It's great in life when we have people around us who know us and can remind us of all the wonderful things we have accomplished. Sometimes however, we are not that fortunate. With that being said, as individuals, it isn't hard to think of the achievements we are proud of. We all have many of them throughout our lives and we do not necessarily equate them to being the foundation for our courage. But if we think about all of our achievements in our lives, especially the ones that we are most proud of, they will have many of the same components. They all required sacrifice, fortitude, perseverance and mental strength. These words are interchangeable when we talk about someone that is courageous. Even Marvin had a hard time finding his point of pride, but to all of us it was pretty obvious. The points of pride that we each have in our lives are obvious too; we just have to remind ourselves of them from time to time.

"How" people understand that courage is in all of us; we have demonstrated it and acted on it. The secret is finding those situations and applying them to our goals.

Again, we often hear people say, *If I can do that, I can do anything.* It couldn't be more true. I am asking you to really embrace this concept, as it will be pivotal for you to continue to do this to gain momentum.

Momentum

When we think of momentum we think of something starting slowly and working up gradually. I think for the most part this is fairly accurate. I believe it's also applicable when you are talking about building courage. Let's face it; there are some things in life that are going to require us to be more courageous than others. We have to build or work up enough courage to do some of these things. This too is okay, and should be expected as we continue through the game of life.

If a person wants to run a marathon, they don't just go out and run 26 miles. They work up to it gradually over time. When the big day comes they will be ready. Courage is no different. You gain momentum through your points of pride, the times when you really had to put your character on the line. Again, it could be anything. It could be standing up to someone that you are intimidated by. It could be making tough or unpopular decisions within your family or organization. Points of pride are very important in being a "How" person because they give us strength and the building block for our courage which helps us develop our character. It is important to use these moments in your life to gain momentum so that you that you will be ready when you need to be courageous.

It's been said, the mind fails before the body. I am a big believer in this. As we discussed earlier, most of us focus on the physical work-up to the race. This is extremely demanding and is a major part of the training. However, we have to believe that we are going to be successful in completing the marathon. Now understandably, it is completely rational and normal to have doubts about our ability to be successful, especially early on. We gain mental strength through accomplishing those tasks that then prepare us for the next.

Courage is derived from passion; passion is derived from things that we care deeply about. If you are not passionate, then you will not have a great deal of desire to rally around your cause. We should not waste time trying to convince ourselves that we are passionate about things when we are not. This will only lead to half-hearted attempts to be successful in that particular endeavor.

The Winds of Change

What do most people have difficulty with in life? You may say such things as speaking in front of a group of people, or confronting another person on a difficult issue. Those are both popular answers. I believe that you can still master your "How" capabilities even without being able to speak in front of large groups of people. Hopefully some of the things that we talked about in the last chapter can help you gain courage to confront difficult people, or talk in front of large groups.

The vast majority of people would agree that the most difficult obstacle in life is change. I think this is because change is often viewed as a negative thing or a consequence. When in fact, it is the only certainty in life;

it's the only thing that we can count on that will happen. Change affects all of us every day throughout our lives. In order to be a true "How" person, you need to learn the art of mastering change.

Change

Change can be such a difficult thing, yet it happens to us everyday and many times throughout the course of a day. Why is it then, that people say they have such a difficult time with change? The other day I woke up to go to work and it was supposed to be a gorgeous spring day, warm with a temperature in the low 70's. That was according to the forecast the night before. I got ready for work that day; I put on a pair of pants and a short-sleeved golf shirt. I was enthused about this great day that we were going to have.

As I was walking out the door, I noticed it seemed to be much colder than the forecasted 55 degrees. It was more like 45 degrees. I thought that it may warm up, so I continued on my way. As I got into my car, I turned on the radio to listen to the *next* weather forecast for the day. A weather front had changed and it was going to bring unseasonably cold weather and possibly rain or snow! Now I was still sitting in the driveway. I had a decision to make; should I go back in and put warmer clothes on or grab a jacket, or should I just tough it out and go? I decided to tough it out and go. The disappointment that I experienced about the weather not being what I had expected lasted all of about ten seconds, and then I was on to thinking about twenty other things.

There were several other things that came up throughout the course of my day that forced me to deal with unexpected changes; there was a detour to get out of my neighborhood, the restaurant that I went to for lunch was out of baked potatoes, the conference call I changed my schedule for was canceled. I bet if you think about just your last couple of days, there have been numerous changes that have occurred, requiring you to change what you were doing or the way you had planned ahead. In these instances, you just make the necessary adjustments and go on. You really don't think too much about it. So I ask you again, why do so many people think they have such a difficult time with change? I think it's because we typically think of change as an unwanted life-altering experience.

In the earlier chapter we talked about perspective, and how different people can look at similar situations and derive different outcomes.

The other day I was scheduled to fly to Chicago to meet a client. Waiting at the airport for more than 2 hours, my flight had been delayed. I was really concerned that I would possibly not make it to my presentation and let my client down. I was talking with the gate agent about alternatives, what time we were expected to takeoff, etc. I am an experienced traveler; I knew that by asking these questions, it wasn't going to get me there any faster. I phoned my client to tell her of the difficulty I was having. She said, "Dan, don't worry about it, you cannot control the weather. We will deal with it when you get here."

I was learning lessons from my client. She was exactly right! Why was I fighting to control what I simply could not? I knew I would feel better if I tried everything I could (if I wasn't going to make it to the presentation on time) and would rest easier knowing my client understood that my absence was out of my control. I am not suggesting that we should just sit by idly and let the winds of change just sweep us wherever they may.

What I am suggesting is that we need to make sure we can decipher between the things we can influence and work to change and to not be so preoccupied with the things that we cannot change.

It's interesting; we typically know when change is going to occur, but not always. Irrespective of whether you know it's coming or not, there is one constant theme in dealing with change; *control what is controllable, and in every case that means you!* "How" people understand that it is difficult to not get mired in all of the change that is affecting them; this is how the victim feelings arise. I am not down-playing this feeling of victimization by change. In some cases, you may actually be victimized by change. However, it does not change the simple fact that you cannot control it. If you get laid off from your job, you can state your case until you are blue in the face as to why that is the wrong decision to your organization. You can be hurt and angry at them, but it still doesn't change your situation.

If you go to the doctor and find out you or one of your family members has a terminal illness, you are surely a victim, but you cannot change the fact that you will have to adapt in a different way, hence change.

I believe this is why people think they have such a huge problem with change. We feel as if we will be victimized by change, so we work to get the resolution that we want. Really, we should be working to positively impact circumstances. However, people typically don't associate "change" as a good thing. Think about it, when one person tells another person they are going through change either personally or professionally, the usual response is "good change?" Even good change is often viewed as bittersweet or necessary. Whatever the rationale, many people really struggle with this concept. In order to be a "How" person, you have to act as a change agent.

What does this mean? Well, it means a few things. You need to feel comfortable with change. Now of course we will not be comfortable with all change or some things that come of change; but you have to realize that change has to happen in order to drive your life and/or organization forward. Change is an abstract movement. When things are working, they are moving; hence change will naturally be created. Some of these things will be beneficial to you and some may not be.

Earlier on we talked about going to the Moon or Marvin learning to walk. These are goals, and all greatness must endure the element of change. If we keep our eyes forward on the goal in which we are trying to achieve, the change that we encounter will be easier to navigate through.

There was a young lady I met a couple of years ago at a conference I attended and I was speaking about change. She stopped me after the presentation and asked me what I thought she should do about a particular situation. She wanted to advance her career, and she had just been presented with a great promotion opportunity in another part of the country. The problem was she had never lived away from home and her whole family still lived in the same town, and the change seemed overwhelming to her. I asked her what made the decision so hard. She said she was torn; she wanted the job but she was scared that she would not be able to acclimate to a new city; she did not know how her parents would react to her moving, etc. I asked her if she had talked to her family about it. She said no.

This was a problem. When we have to make decisions that will alter our lives to some degree, we need to question. We have to ask ourselves, do we have all of the facts or as many as we can to weigh the pros and cons? It is difficult to make educated and informed decisions about change without all of the facts. She was worrying about what her parents might think. My suggestion on that point was to simply ask them. However, when you ask someone for their perspective, don't be discouraged if it runs in contrast to yours.

I asked her why she was interested in the move. She said it was something she dreamt about since she was young. She dreamed of being an executive, and that would never happen in her small town. The town was too small and didn't have enough industry to make that kind of opportunity real. Essentially, she was at a cross road; the only way to accomplish her goal was to move. So when you take all of the emotion out of the equation, the correct decision was to move. I am not saying that emotional reasoning won't be overwhelming in making decisions; I am saying the exact opposite. You have to extrapolate the emotion out, through perspective, optimism, and courage.

First, she had to understand her motivation. She had a clear understanding of what she wanted and why she was doing what she was doing and how hard she was going to have to work at it. Second, she had to look at it from differing angles (perspective). What's the worst thing that could happen? She could move to a new city and she could have an awful experience. She could be homesick and miserable and only want to come home. In that event, she could always come home. She can return to her hometown where she is comfortable and knows that she is happy. Third, she needed to be optimistic about what she was doing. By looking at it through the perspective I just mentioned, it acts as a safety net. When you are making these kinds of decisions, ask yourself, *what is the worst thing that could happen?* Then answer the question. You will probably be surprised as to how manageable the worst possible thing that could happen to you is.

Make sure that you pepper your decision with realistic optimism. We can surmise that if she were to go, and hate it, she would not be any worse off than she already was. But, what if she loved it? What if the experience was far richer than she could have imagined? She meets many wonderful people, and expands her horizons. As far as courage goes, it's a win-win. If you go and it doesn't work, well you went; you will never wonder, *what if?* You will have pushed your comfort limits and for that you are always better off and will forever be stronger from the experience. If it works out, great! This point of pride can be used to explore new horizons and help build the strength to conquer other difficult decisions.

When you look at change in life, it is hardly ever as bad as you may initially think.

It surely wasn't for this young lady and the same can be true for you.

Attacking Change

Earlier I talked about being victimized. What I mean by this is sometimes we feel like things are happening around us and we are just going to have to wait and see what happens and then deal with it. "How" people do not have this perspective at all.

Life is not a chess game; you can't wait and see what others are going to do and then react to the things that have already happened. If you live that way, you will constantly be a victim because you will always be on your heels waiting to see what is going to happen to you. "How" people engage change! If you are not happy at work and you hear there may be downsizing, an "If" person would wait to see what happens and have the perspective that they will deal with whatever happens. A "How" person would be getting their resume out, they would be interviewing, and they would be creating opportunities. Change is coming, one way or another. Make your move. Let people react to what you have set as your objective. The difference is that the "How" person is taking control, hence affecting change instead of being effected by it. When we do this in the majority of cases, we have a better change experience than if we wait until we are forced to change.

I was talking with my friend the other day and he was having continuous problems with his car. He kept saying he would get a new one when this car finally died. Well guess what? His car died on a Tuesday morning; the same day he was supposed to take the kids to daycare because his wife was traveling for the week. He had a household to run and that required a lot of driving. He had to go through the initial expense of renting a car, and then didn't have time to look for a new car because he was looking after his family that week. He was scattered. By the time he went to look for a new car he was desperate, and needed to buy one immediately. Now he feels that he didn't really get what he wanted; he overpaid and is stuck with a car that he never wanted in the first place.

He knew that change was coming. Had he attacked it and been more proactive, he would have been prepared and not only maximized his old vehicle's value (instead of running it into the ground) he would've had a plan in place when his car eventually expired.

I played football for many years, and when I was little I remember being a little "gun shy" about hitting or being hit by another player. My father told me something that was very impactful about playing football, but now I think it's even more impactful as we look at attacking change. I was scared of getting hurt when I would make contact with another player. My father said, "It doesn't matter how fast he is coming at you, or how big he is, the only time you will get hurt is when you don't hit him with everything that you have."

In football, if you want to play, you are going to get hit. In life we are going to get hit too, by change. The only time we are going to get hurt is when we don't attack change with everything that we have.

Setback-The Real Question

I have made quite a few assumptions as I have written this book. Well, I am going to make a guarantee to you. If you have been good at everything you have ever done, up to this point in your life, you have never experienced heartbreak, setback or defeat. Prepare yourself because setback is inevitable.

We all have to deal with a modest amount of setback throughout our lives, some more than others. I once read a quote that stated, "If your life has no failures, you are not taking enough risks." It is true! It's kind of like the old gambling saying, "You have to bet big to win big!" You can only win a proportional amount based on how much you bet.

This is an important concept! In a lot of self improvement books, you will read that the author advocates taking risk. I however, am not concerned with the amount of risk that you take. I don't think you have to be an enormous risk taker to be a "How" person. I think you are better off if you understand the relationship between risk and reward. Furthermore, I believe you have to understand the relationship between having a dream and the enormous elation and growth that you can experience by perusing it.

Life is like poker; the only difference is that in life you cannot fold. You have to play the hands you are dealt. In some cases, the most exciting poker-wins have come from hands in which the player felt compelled to play based on his or her standing and current situation in the game. Obviously you know you will not win all of the time and there may be many instances when loosing (or experiencing setback in life) seems to happen more frequently than you expect; but how exciting is it when that hand wins! You have to play to win! In life you have no choice but to play, and to "How" people, we welcome every hand as a challenge to attack. This is when you will experience the most personal growth. Understanding and welcoming change as a "How" person will help you take what may look like a bad situation in life, and turn it into something incredible.

My father was scheduled to have a fairly routine heart bypass operation several years ago. At first, everything went fine with the surgery. He was up and alert and talking with my mother, my sister and me. I thought everything was under control, so at my father's urging, I booked a flight and headed home. A couple of days went by and they were rather uneventful. I would call and check in and things seemed to be fine. At this point, I took a deep sigh of relief thinking we were going to get through this. On the third morning after the surgery, I called and couldn't reach anyone. I wasn't overly concerned because things had been progressing well. After several calls, my sister answered and said, "Danny, he has taken a turn for the worse, we are not sure what has happened, the doctors are trying to stabilize him." My heart dropped; I was hundreds of miles away and I felt completely helpless! This was the hand I was dealt.

I quickly made arrangements to get back to my family as soon as possible. My sister then informed me that she and my mother spoke with the doctor. The doctor told them there was a chance my father would not make it out of the hospital. Needless to say, we were all very distraught. On my flight, I was having a myriad of emotions. How would I react to seeing my father in a completely different state than when I left? Would I be able to be strong for my sister and mother? Was my dad going to die? I was 36 years old and for the first time in my life, I needed to deal with a situation like an adult. I truly struggled with this hand I was dealt. It was one I was not ready for but was forced to *deal with* or "play."

I thought about how my father first wound up in the hospital. He had to make a choice, to either have immediate open heart surgery or not. The chance of survival was an extreme risk and concern because of some of his health issues. The reward was the obvious, living a longer, healthier life. My mother and father had mixed emotions about what to do. The end result was, if he didn't do it, he was a ticking bomb; he may live 30 more years, he may live 3 more days. My dad decided that was no way to live.

We all have had to calculate the relationship between doing something along with the positives and negatives that could be a result of the decision. In fact, we do this on a micro scale everyday. But sometimes some decisions are more complex than others and they contribute to more consequences. Some examples could be the decision to buy property or to invest heavily in something (i.e. starting your own business), starting or ending a relationship, etc. As Buzz Aldren said, "The hardest part is deciding to go!"

When we decide to go, we have to be committed and follow through with our choice! If we are not sure, then we should evaluate and make sure we are absolute. When we experience setback in pursuit of a goal, we can not abandon our goal. There will inevitably be setbacks. This is when and only when we can possibly fail. Once you give up or quit, you have failed. As "How" people, we will never fail, because we will not give up or quit. We may not always accomplish what we set out to do, but we remain committed to our goal.

During the American Revolution, our army was on their heels. They lost just about every major battle they were engaged in. Our troops were tired and weary and wanted to return to their families. As many of you know, the winter of 1776 at Valley Forge was a very trying time. Our fragile revolution was on its final legs and all but broken. It was setback after setback. However, as easy as it would have been to surrender and accept defeat due to the lack of necessary supplies to fight, and our soldiers' spirits at the cusp of being broken, General George

Washington would not surrender. On a last ditch effort, General Washington crossed the Delaware River on Christmas night and attacked British outposts. This was the turning point in the war.

People often rhetorically ask *What if we wouldn't have defeated the Hessians during the Battle of Trenton?* The question is not, "What if we were unsuccessful at the Battle of Trenton?" The question is, "What if George Washington would have abandoned his goal?" The point is that success and failure are often only a fraction of a decision apart. You won't know if you don't try, and because Washington tried, we will never have to wonder what *if* we wouldn't have been successful in Trenton. It would have been easy to throw in the towel and say this is all too much, we just can't compete, and we can't win. Had Washington done this, we would have never given democracy the opportunity to flourish and we would have never become the wonderful nation we are today.

My dad decided to have the surgery; he decided *to go*. His decision *to go* had a much different result than that of our nation's conquest for the Moon. After surgery my father needed to be put on a respirator. Every day it was touch-and-go due to complications from the surgery. Each day presented a new medical challenge. I remember talking with one of the doctors and he was explaining a particular procedure he could perform on my father. He stated, "The risk is, it could make him much worse. The reward is it could make him much better." He then went on to explain further complications if the procedure did not go well. This put my mother into a state of complete dismay and despair. I knew I had to think differently than my mother and sister and manage this very difficult situation, regardless of what was going to happen with my father.

In that next minute, with the doctor, my mother, and sister in the room I said, "Look we can only deal with the situation at hand. We cannot be concerned about what might or might not happen. We have to make the best decisions we can at the moment in time we have to make them."

Life is no different. "How" people understand that after you make the decision to go, there is no going back. You decided for a reason; stay honest and clear eyed about why you made that decision and deal with the obstacles when they arise. When we experience setback, we have to do a couple of things:

Focus on what we can control. Often we get preoccupied thinking and worrying about things that are beyond our control. We must put those things out of our mind and make decisions that could provide a positive outcome. After we make that decision we will deal with the next set of circumstances, whatever they may be. We talked earlier about the fact that fear can be paralyzing. It can also be overwhelming! "How" people understand that it is okay to be afraid, but we still have to act—we have to make decisions and work to solidify a positive outcome. It's the "If" people that ask, *what if this, what if that?* "How" people say, *how do I make this as good as it can possibly be?* Again, "How" gives us command and confidence. "If" breeds insecurity and a lack of confidence.

Be decisive—make decisions. I firmly believe that it is better to be decisive and make decisions and work to control your fate, instead of letting fate control you. This doesn't mean you will make every right decision, often we will not know if a decision was "right" until much time has passed. I do, however, believe we make no wrong decisions in life. Think about it; your life has turned out okay. Sure there are always things you wish were a little different, but on whole it's good. If you look back throughout your life, I bet it's safe to say you regret decisions you made to *not* do certain things. You regret the things that you *didn't do*, not the things you *did*.

As difficult as setbacks are, when we put our heart and effort into something, even if we come up short of our goal, we are better off and further ahead because of the experience. Often, some of our best achievements come in the pursuit of a goal or dream. As we discussed earlier, what if we wouldn't have reached our goal of getting to the Moon before 1970? The world would not have ended; but sure, we would have been disappointed. We are so much better off because we decided to go! Think of all of the technologies that were invented. I actually read the other day that the Smart phone, which many of us use today, comprises more technology than what we used to put men on the Moon. We would have never progressed at the rate we have if we didn't test and push ourselves to chase our dream.

"How" people understand the journey is just as important, if not more important than the destination. It's what we gain in search of our goals and dreams that gives us the future tools to achieve even greater feats. It's fulfilling when we achieve what we set out to accomplish, and often we will. However, sometimes we will not!

My father survived his ordeal he had a few years back. He has since regained his health, changed his much needed diet, and is probably in the best shape of his adult life. I sometimes want to ask myself, *what if he would have died in that hospital*. But that's not the right question. The correct question is *what if my father decided to not have the surgery?* Considering the track he was on, I am quite confident he wouldn't be here today. Just like the young lady that was making the decision to transfer, or Geroge Washington deciding to cross the Delaware River, these individuals gave themselves the chance to succeed. Had they decided not to take a risk or *to go*, they would have been no worse off than they already were, nor would they be any better!

Playing to Win

I was watching a football game one afternoon. The announcers began the pregame by talking about one of the teams and what a dominant offensive line this team had, specifically the left side of their offensive line. So as you can imagine, the team began by running the ball to the left side. They repeated this, play after play, throughout the game. As the game progressed the commentators continued to talk about the line as the strength of this team.

Interestingly enough, as good as this component of the team was, they still lost the football game. After the game and for the entire next week, the Press hounded the coach and the players. The fans were upset with the lack of play calling, the same plays over and over again etc,

etc. Everyone had an opinion about the game plan and the decisions to run the ball repeatedly. I recall seeing one Press conference where the coach was being hassled about the play calling. The coach said something very important. He said, "We played in a manner and fashion that would give us the best shot at winning." Now this was important, because I don't think the fans and or the media were thrilled with his response, but it made a lot of sense. The coach understood that this option was the strongest attribute of his team; and that in order to win or at least have a chance, the team had to do what they do well and do it even better. That made a lot more sense than to try to execute a game plan that was not consistent with his team's strengths, and hope that all of a sudden the players were going to perfect a weakness *and* do it so well, that they would be victorious!

From a young age we are always taught to "be better." This typically means, work on the things you do not do well. Here is an example – if a student is getting an A in English and an F in Math, what subject do you think the parents are going to tutor their child in? Well, obviously you can't accept an F, but what if it was a C? My point is, is that we always look to improve on a lacking attribute.

At first blush, why wouldn't the parents think about how they can develop their child's English skills? It's easy, because the thought is *they are good at English, and don't need to give it any additional attention.* I can bet this student is not going to be an accountant. The point is, is that from an early age we are funneled to put time and effort into underperforming attributes instead of working to expand and grow the ones we are good at. The parents are not thinking about developing the strengths in their child because they too were taught to develop upon their own weaknesses. This is also reinforced in their adult life in their personal and professional relationships.

We have to understand that the things we don't do well may improve through hard work and dedication, but they are only going to improve to a mediocre level. This is a simple concept of the human psyche; we enjoy the things we are good at, we don't enjoy the things we are not good at. If you don't enjoy doing something, how dedicated are you really going to be to improving it? Again, remember motivation is the driver of effort and effort is the predictor of success. You will never be as successful as you could be if you are not truly motivated to do what you are doing. You will never be motivated if you don't find satisfaction from what you are doing.

It's funny to me that some of the top business organizations in the world haven't grasped this concept yet! How many of you have been through some performance review process and they indicate your strengths and weaknesses? Or in some cases, just your weaknesses. Then, from the review process, a "plan" is put together for you to improve on your weaknesses. I don't think there is a more devastating or bigger waste of time than an exercise like this, that an employer can put an employee through. I understand that we will always have to work at rounding out some of the things we need to work on. That is a fact of life. But clearly, we get to where we are and experience the success that we do because of our strengths *not* our opportunities. Yet, we spend so much time working on the things that will only get marginally better, hence you are limiting your ability to maximize your true potential. Furthermore, you're not spending time developing the skill sets you have already, which can get increasingly better. So in this case, it's a double whammy! You are not making your strengths bigger strengths, and you are exerting time and energy on something that can only improve minimally. The other interesting thing about developing weaknesses is, the second you are not subjected to the individuals or organizations that are asking you to work on these attributes, you stop doing it. Why? Because you don't like it! However, you will always resort to your strengths!

We are motivated to perform our strengths. When we go on a job interview, do we talk about how bad our opportunities are? Of course not! And when you get hired, it's because the company is excited about all of the strengths you will bring to the role and the organization, not your areas of weakness that the company will need to help you fix.

You will always be better and perform better in your areas of strength. This is the roadmap to your personal and professional success. "How" people resist the thought of spending time lamenting and putting volumes of effort into developing our weaknesses. "How" people also carry this same perspective to their teams and organizations.

"How" people recognize their strengths and they utilize those strengths to attain success. "How" people also understand the strengths of their coworkers, especially those working as a team and they leverage those strengths to reach success. I feel that when we are presented with an objective or a task, before we engage it, we need to take some time and inventory of our strengths and how we can leverage them to attain ultimate success; or give ourselves and our teams the best chance for success.

I was working with an organization and their sales team. In this organization they had eight sales professionals throughout the country. Each sales person was responsible for all sales activity in that territory. If an opportunity was in his or her territory, they would handle all aspects of the sales process including, client relationships, proposal development, presentations, etc. This is how most sales teams are organized. They asked me to work with them to improve the organization's sales figures. I attended the first team meeting to get an understanding of the team and their perspectives.

The first thing the Executive Vice President of Sales did was put up a list of all of the bids they had *lost* and wanted to have a group discussion around what they could have done better. I had to stop her! I'm not sure there was any more negative way to start a meeting! I proposed that we put up all of the bids that were *won* and talk about why they won them. After everyone quit looking at me like I had three heads, we did exactly that. The only problem was, they were not sure why they won when they did! They never asked the clients, *why did you choose us?*

They did not have a consultant doing post mortem debriefs with the clients on the accounts they won. Ironically enough, they had all of that information on the accounts they lost. Think about that! This company (as many do) spent tens of thousands of dollars on consultant fees, the same in man hours trying to figure out what they did wrong. Look, it's important to know why you lost, but it's ten times more important to know why you won!

Organizations are like people. They have personalities and sometimes those personalities don't mesh well with other organizations. No one in that room was going to change that. But when you demonstrate strength over the competition, you must further develop that strength so you can capitalize on it. Again, the same philosophy we all have ingrained in us; figure out what we don't do well. This bleeds into our organizations. "How" people stop this nonsense. I understand we have to spend some time examining why we did not do as well as we would have liked to. However, I am suggesting we spend more time figuring out why we were better than the competition and spend our time and energies making ourselves more dominant.

What if Marvin would have sat around thinking about all of the things that he did wrong and spent hours

87

and hours, days upon days thinking about those things? Well, actually he did. To his own admission, it made him angry, resentful and he only focused on the negative. This was the same thing this sales team was being asked to do, and it happens throughout corporations and organizations today. They spend so much time looking back. How is that going to help you? You understand where you made mistakes and I agree that's important, but how much time do we really spend analyzing why we are successful? Not much really. And this is why I say not much; because I can almost assure you, in your life and the organizations you are a part of, you have spent more time thinking about the mistakes you made, rather than the successes you've earned.

As the planning process continued, I asked the group to rate each other based on individual strengths; there was no discussion around any weaknesses. In other words, who wrote the best proposals, did the best presentations, etc. Interestingly enough, when the team members rated each other, the ratings aligned with what each person recognized as their own individual strength. I knew there was no better way to instill confidence in someone's ability than when a group of your peers designates your strengths. Also, in every case, the strengths that were conveyed were the parts of the job the individual enjoyed most. Again, we like what we are good at.

Over time, we changed the mechanics of the organization. We had each sales representative become more involved in a specific aspect of ALL of the bids that designated their strength. In other words, John was great at presentations. He would work with all of the teams before they had to do a presentation. He would drive or fly to meet a team, coach and help them develop the appropriate message. This activity was mirrored for all aspects of the bid process. Madison was a great proposal writer; she would work to make sure all proposals carried the right message and were centric to the client's needs. The important factor in doing this was we had team members focused on their strength and what they enjoyed doing. They did not feel anxiety because they were not being asked to perform tasks they knew were not their strong suit.

We also changed the commission structure. The commissions were now paid as the result of the team, not any one individual. So when the team succeeded, everyone succeeded. Through this process, we broke down silos, fostered a new team orientated approach and increased new business revenue by 45%.

The bottom line is we focused on what we do well, put our best players in situations where they perform the best and achieved superior results.

As individuals we need to do the same thing. I am asking you to spend some time thinking about what you are good at and how you can make that better. If you enjoy writing, take an additional writing class. If you enjoy public speaking, join Toastmasters. Whatever the case, you are going to be chosen for something because you are superior at a certain skill set. A skill set ultimately becomes superior when you start off with doing something you are good at. You enjoy it, continue to engage it, work hard, and eventually master that skill. I have yet to find an individual who has taken a substandard skill set and made it superior and sustained it. Your strengths sustain you, your opportunities will not.

Earlier I was talking about a football team that played to their strengths and lost. The next week they did the exact same thing and won. All of the critics were silenced and *now* the fans thought the coach was brilliant. We are not always going to achieve the level of success that we desire, but it is about giving yourself the strongest chance that you will. That year the team only had two losses. They never changed the strategy of playing to their strength. In life we have to do the same thing. Don't worry so much about what you don't do well; focus on what you do well. Dominate in the areas that you truly can dominate in and success will surely follow.

A Supporting Cast

In life, we can change just about anything we want; and clearly, there are some things that we will not be able to change. Earlier we talked about focusing on the things you can change and not spending much energy worrying about the things you cannot.

"How" people realize the pursuit of any dream or objective can not be done alone. We have to surround ourselves with people who will support our ideas and our vision and appreciate our strengths. This is true if we are working to accomplish an individual objective or lead a team to accomplish a goal. Often in life, we spend far too much time trying to convince others why we are right and or trying to change their perception.

When I worked in business development, I spent a lot of time trying to convince potential customers that the service I was providing was far superior to the one they were currently utilizing. Now there is nothing wrong with this; this is a huge component of sales. However, I spent countless hours spending time doing this with potential customers that had no openness what-so-ever to what I was saying. But I thought, *I am a great salesman, I will convince them.* As good as I thought I was, do you know how many times I convinced a customer to make a change when they were not honestly open to what I was saying? Zero! Not even once! So really, these people weren't even potential customers. I should have never wasted time calling on them again. This was a valuable lesson in life, because these types of clients were making me question my sales ability.

The problem was not with my sales ability; it was their inability to be open minded! There was nothing I could say or do that was ever going to change their mind. So it was a waste of time, I was never going to be successful. In order to be a "How" person, we must surround ourselves with individuals that are open to our goal or pursuit. This doesn't mean whatever you say, they are just going to get onboard with; it means they have decided to not be closed minded to your thoughts or goals. Sometimes in life people are happy with the way things are or have views and opinions they are unwilling to change. This is okay. In fact, it's great if their views coincide with your hopes and aspirations. However, it's fatal if the views do not align. You will be wasting time trying to get support or "buy-in" on your objectives if they are never willing to entertain your ambition. Often times an individual will tell you that they are open and supportive, but there is a sure way to tell – their behavior!

I know of a family, where a mother had raised her three sons and wanted to re-enter the workforce after several years of being home. Throughout her children's lives she remained loyal and dedicated to being a stay-at-home mom while her husband went to work everyday in order to provide monetarily for the family. Now that her sons reached an age where they could be self sufficient and didn't need as much of her attention, she wanted a job outside of the home. When she mentioned this idea to her husband, his initial reaction was, "You don't need to work." She tried to explain that it wasn't a matter of necessity. It was because she wanted to set a goal of getting a job and work to accomplish it. After months of these conversations, her husband finally agreed that he would be supportive of his wife's endeavors. However, every time she tried to do something to better herself, he would come up with a reason as to why she could not do it. In one instance, she was thinking about taking a position with hours in the evening. Her husband's response was, "Who will take the boys to practice?" In another situation, she was approached by an entrepreneur about a business opportunity. Her husband said, "That is just a get-rich quick scheme; that's not good." Whatever the case, he had a reason every time to challenge his wife, telling her why she *shouldn't* do what she wanted to.

Well here is a wake up call! As "How" people, we need to focus on doing what we know we should. We can all find reasons why we *shouldn't* do something, but we need to start focusing on what we *should* do. We do not need other people to influence us negatively. We are completely capable of making decisions by ourselves. Every time the wife would ask her husband why he was not being supportive, he would say, "I am, I told you I support you with this." That was true in what he said, but that's not what his behavior showed. Look, it's difficult enough to navigate the waters of life and accomplish our goals, but it is almost impossible when you have to row a boat full of other individuals that are unwilling to pick up an oar and help! Her husband was unwilling to pick up an oar and help her accomplish her goal. By him not doing so created resentment on her part. She did ultimately accomplish her goal but their relationship was never the same.

There are many reasons why people are "blockers" to our goals and objectives, and I could write volumes as to how to deal with these people and why they feel the way they do. For the sake of right now, if the people you need to be supportive of your goals and dreams are not "open" to helping you achieve them, we need to move away from them. As I mentioned earlier, I was never successful in convincing someone who was not open to making a change, to make one.

Marvin had to surround himself with the people in his life that would foster and nourish his ambition to get his life back to where he wanted it. Not that we will never accomplish our goals if we are surrounded by people that do not support them, but it makes it 100 times more difficult. Marvin was going to have a hard enough time learning to walk, run and get his life back together in total. Why would he want to be surrounded by people he had to convince what we wanted was the right thing? He wouldn't!

We will always find people that will hold us back or convey negative energy towards our hopes and dreams. "How" people don't listen to them, nor do they try to convince or persuade them. "How" people surround themselves with a supporting cast of individuals that want to see them succeed.

When President Kennedy decided to go to the Moon, do you think NASA rounded up all of the people that were convinced that this could never be done and put the country's hopes and aspirations in them? Of course not!

Sometimes we have to be honest about where we stand with other individuals in our life. We might have to make tough decisions to separate ourselves from unsupportive people because they don't provide the true support, physically and emotionally that we need to accomplish our goals. It is important to remember that our success, in large part, will correlate to the people that we surround ourselves with, and so will our failures.

I was working for an organization with the same boss for a few years and I was known to consistently have very good results with my sales figures. Unfortunately when

I met my new boss, our first couple of interactions were not very good. I had a run-in with a particular client and my new boss felt that I should have handled it differently. The end result was the client was not happy and my boss began forming a particular opinion of me. From that point on, he would take situations that really had nothing to do with our first interaction and somehow tie them in to it; hence he created a skill deficiency in me. The deficiency in his mind was that I did not respond adequately to clients' needs. The irony was, I sold millions of dollars every year, and every year I was the top sales producer in the organization. It would be very difficult to do this if I did not respond adequately to clients' needs. Now I did have areas I needed to improve on, and even outlined them for my boss during my review process. I felt that my ability to respond to clients needs was one of my stronger attributes. I felt this was evidenced in the relationships I built and the quantifiable sales figures I provided for the organization. This is where the problem came in. No matter what I did, no matter how hard I worked to prove to my boss that I responded adequately to clients' needs, he was never going to be open to me being able to do that. I spent years trying to convince him of this. What ultimately happened was my confidence started to suffer and I started to believe I actually had an issue responding to clients needs! I also started questioning what my boss thought of me. I asked myself questions like, *How should I handle this? How can I convince him I am doing the right thing?*

The problem was I was never going to convince him. My numbers dropped due to my lack of confidence and a paralyzing fear around trying to do the right thing, and this reinforced his perception of me. Needless to say it took me a long time to realize that my career was over with this organization; not because of my ability, but because my boss was closed minded. I wasted over two years of my life trying to gain a client that was never going to be open to what I was selling. In this case the client was my boss. I should have recognized this much sooner.

When people are nay-sayers and closed minded, "How" people understand that we have to make the decision to surround ourselves with others that are open and supportive to the goals that we are working to accomplish.

"How" people surround themselves with other "How" people.

My close friend was going through a divorce; this was a divorce that he did not want. He was trying everything he could to keep the relationship together. However, his wife didn't have the same drive to work on the relationship. As hard as he tried, it was impossible for him to try hard enough for both of them. The fact of the matter was that she no longer wanted this partnership of marriage. This was a very difficult thing for my friend to grasp, and it took time. However, he gradually understood that he could not make someone be somewhere or do something if they did not want to. He was then able to take the energy he was wasting and funnel it to something much more positive. In this case, it was his children. His relationship with his kids had became stronger through the divorce. He admits this never would have happened if he had continued to focus energy towards a hopeless cause.

A great example of trying to force people to rally around a cause or an effort in which their heart is not really there, is the Vietnam War. Regardless of what your personal feelings are about our involvement in Vietnam, there are some valuable facts that we can learn from this war. As I discussed earlier, regardless if it's a divorce or an organizational objective, you can not make people get on board with your objective. The majority of American people did not want us to be engaged in the Vietnam War; and it ultimately crippled our Nation's morale since as we all know, we exited Vietnam several years later in defeat. There are many factors that make the Vietnam War different from all of our other wars. It was the most polarizing; the only one where the outrage for the war, in many cases, was directed at our own troops who were sent to Vietnam to fight (many, not by their choosing). Interestingly enough, if you look at all of the wars beginning with the American Revolution through present day, when we have had our civilian public in support of our troops fighting overseas (not necessarily the cause) we have been successful.

We have to surround ourselves with people that want the same things in life and in business that we do. Of course, there are always going to be disagreements and differences in opinion, but directionally, we have to surround ourselves with people that believe, or those who are at least open to the endeavors we want to pursue.

Becoming a "How" Person

I t is true, the day I met Marvin truly changed my life forever. That chance encounter has taken me on a journey through my thoughts, my views, and my perspectives of being successful in life. The one thing that I keep coming back to is *we* are ultimately responsible for our *own* success. I am sure you have heard that many times throughout your life too. After meeting Marvin and reflecting on some of the many stories I have shared with you throughout this book, there is something more apparent to me than ever. We are in control of our mental outlook and in control of our own destiny.

I think the difference between a fulfilled life and an unfulfilled life is that we all have to embrace the simple fact that each one of us can accomplish great things. And

to each one of us great things may mean something totally different. When we think in terms of "How," we are
energized and accountable to accomplish these things.

Often the only thing that stands between us and our
dreams is us. It is difficult to find the confidence and
fortitude to make decisions that will lead us to success.
The fear of failure can be greater than the excitement of
succeeding. We essentially stand in our own way because
we allow ourselves to live in the world of "If." "If" is the
easy way. "If" is the safe way. "If" allows the winds of
destiny to take us where they may.

There are "If" people and there are "How" people.
You are either one or the other. You are either the person
who will accomplish and lead others to do great things
or you will forever be sitting, watching passively and
cynically, while great things are accomplished by others.
You should also understand that at any moment you can
decide to be a "How" person. Just because you haven't
thought that way before doesn't mean you can't start
thinking that way now. "How" people are those who
believe our best days are ahead of us, and greatness lies
within each one of us. "How" people understand that
there should be no fear in setting and striving for a goal

or an objective, because even if we come up short, we are better after than we were before we started.

Success comes from "How." "How" is a powerful word. "How" is so powerful that it took our country to the Moon when the odds were stacked completely against us. "How" has helped to create many other successes as evidenced by this book. "How" will guide you on your road to success. You just have to decide, are you a "How" person?

"How" people realize that we have to be motivated, and we have to know why we are doing something. This is the foundation of our success. You can only fake doing something for so long until the resentment of doing it will consume you, like it did Marvin. When you become resentful, you begin to view the world through a negative perspective. Marvin was motivated because he wanted a better life for himself and for his family; his line of thought with regard to motivation was clear.

We also understand that the more motivated we are, the more effort we are going to put towards accomplishing our goal. The more effort we put towards our goal, the better outcomes we will have. Each person's motivation is unique. "How" people will not be deterred because other individuals think their rationale is flawed. Many of us have motivation to do the same things as others, but for different reasons. The important thing is that we are motivated and we understand why we are making the decisions we make.

When President Kennedy declared that we should attempt to get to the Moon before the end of the decade, he was not overcome with worry and the fact that the United States only had 15 minutes and 22 seconds of manned space flight. I bet in his mind, the 15 minutes and 22 seconds was better than 10 minutes and 14 seconds.

"How" people understand bad things that will happen to us sometimes. It is what we take away from those bad situations that will make or break our efforts in accomplishing our goals. Just like the people in the grocery store looking through the tomatoes, no one accepted the first tomato they picked up. It did not matter if there were 200 or 20 tomatoes; each person still took away the best tomatoes they could find. Some of the individuals took away better tomatoes than others, but it's the way all of the individuals accepted that no matter what their situation, the tomato they walked away with was the best of the bunch. "How" people understand that it will not always be easy to find differing perspectives to make these bad situations or events easier to deal with. However, "How" people understand that the things we take from challenging or difficult situations, or really the things that we accept from these circumstances, will give us greater ability to deal with them. "How" people understand the importance of perspective. This will enable them to conceive optimism, and that realistic optimism is crucial to capitalizing on negative situations. From realistic optimism, we generate a contagious spirit. Others want to be part of something imaginative and great. It's the "How" people that find paths around and through tough times when it may seem completely hopeless. "How" people are the ones that will ascend the ranks of our organizations and communities.

"How" people realize that a necessary trait of anyone who is going to lead themselves or others is courage. "How" people understand that courage is made, it is not a virtue that you are born with. Courage is in all of us and we just need to know where to find it. "How" people will capitalize on their previous points of pride throughout their life. These points of pride are the times when "How" people have achieved a goal or an objective that was important to them. Like we learned from

Beth, sometimes these points of pride are tests and accomplishments that we do not even view internally as such. Again, courage is in all of us, we just have to look for it; and then, through transference, we need to apply the same principles to the test we are faced with.

Momentum is another characteristic of "How" people. We understand that sometimes we have to work up courage in order to face a significant challenge. Like running a race, you start with shorter workouts and work up to larger ones. The same is true for courage. Our points of pride that have given us strength and a self respect should be utilized to build even larger points of pride for ourselves. In doing this, we are creating momentum. As your courage builds, and momentum fuels it, there will be no challenge that will make you look the other way.

"How" people understand that there is one constant in life – and that's change. It will happen to all of us. "How" people understand that change can be an intimidating thing. "How" people realize the best way to accept change is to attack it and to not allow ourselves to be victimized by it, hence being intimidating by it. We feel change is taking place and we have no control over what is happening or going to happen to us. "How" people are those who welcome change because they are creating it. "How" people are going to do the things in their lives that will mitigate the chance to be victimized by change. Sure, there are going to be times in all of our lives when change is going to be cast upon us. In these situations, "How" people remember that they can only control themselves and not all of the circumstances around them.

Like the young woman I met at the conference who was contemplating moving. "How" people take the emotion out of making decisions that will incorporate change. We do this by asking ourselves, *what's the worst thing that could happen?* When we do this, we find that the change is not as significant as we may think it is.

"How" people understand that life is like poker. The only difference is that in the game of life we do not get to fold any of the hands we are dealt. Sometimes when we are dealt bad hands, we are dealt setback. Again, like we discussed, we can not throw in the bad hands. "How" people understand when we are dealt setback we have to do the following things:

Focus on what we can control. Often we get preoccupied thinking and worrying about things that are beyond our control. We must put those things out of our mind and make decisions that could provide a positive outcome. After we make that decision we will deal with the next set of circumstances, whatever they may be. We talked earlier about the fact that fear can be paralyzing. It can also be overwhelming! "How" people understand that it is okay to be afraid, but we still have to act—we have to make decisions and work to solidify a positive outcome. It's the "If" people that ask, *what if this, what if that?* "How" people say, *how do I make this as good as it can possibly be?* Again, "How" gives us command and confidence. "If" breeds insecurity and a lack of confidence.

Be decisive—make decisions. I firmly believe that it is better to be decisive and make decisions and work to control your fate, instead of letting fate control you. This doesn't mean you will make every right decision, often we will not know if a decision was "right" until much time has passed. I do, however, believe we make no wrong decisions in life. Think about it; your life has turned out okay. Sure there are always things you wish were a little different, but on whole it's good. If you look back throughout your life, I bet it's safe to say you regret decisions you made to *not* do certain things. You regret the things that you *didn't do*, not the things you *did*.

"How" people realize that all of us have talents and we all have things that we may not do so well. "How" people fight societal norms of asking people to work on their weaknesses and try to develop them into strengths. 'How" people understand that we have to embrace and maximize our own strengths as well as the strengths of the individuals' in our organizations. Our strengths are why we experience successes, not because of our weaknesses.

We need to spend more time on why we experienced success and not waste so much time on why we were not successful. It is important to understand why we don't do as well as we would like to sometimes, but our focus needs to be redirected to the positive for future successes.

We have to surround ourselves with other "How" people. The voyage to complete our goals and dreams can be done alone, but it is far more difficult. The extra energy and effort that you will have to exert trying to convince others to support your goal can be exhausting and sometimes even devastating. Sometimes in life we are going to encounter individuals that are set in their ways and are not open to your thoughts or way of think- ing, hence they probably will not be supportive of your goals. "How" people resist the urge to try to persuade these individuals to be supportive of their cause. "How" people simply separate themselves from these individuals. Again, these people will not be shunned from our lives; we just shouldn't have to defend our motivation to anyone. Remember, our motivation is like our fingerprint. It is unique to each one of us.

Living through *The Power of How* will not always be easy. We all loose our resolve sometimes. Our lives will be determined largely by how we view ourselves and our ability to achieve greatness. As I said in the beginning of this book, believing is not always easy. We all have the power to make decisions that will make our journey what we want it to be. As you go forward as a "How" person, I hope you embrace and continue to foster the same "How" culture that so many accomplished individuals and lived by and provided us the roadmap for personal success.

It is truly amazing that a 15-minute chance encounter with a young man at a gas station caused me to do the soul searching that I did. And continue to do, to this day. I fundamentally believe that every person on this earth wants to accomplish greatness; again greatness is a relative term and is unique to each individual. I do not believe that anyone wakes up in the morning and says, *how can I live an unfulfilled life?* But life is hard for all of us. I thought when I met Marvin, he had it pretty bad.

The difference is, he did not. As I said at the beginning of this chapter, we are ultimately responsible for our own success; and in my view, success comes down to one simple word – happiness. We all want and deserve to be happy. If we are not, then "How" can we be happy? Again it's not a matter of "If," it's a matter of "How."

Made in the USA
Columbia, SC
25 February 2018